Space Junk

A play for children and anyone still young enough to have a dream

Les Ellison

A Samuel French Acting Edition

SAMUELFRENCH-LONDON.CO.UK
SAMUELFRENCH.COM

Copyright © 1999 by Samuel French Ltd (book)
Songs: The Wonder of it All, Volga's Song, Re-Entry Song
Copyright © 1999 by Cheryl
Lowery and Kirsty Body (music and lyrics). Space Junk Song
Copyright © 1999 by Samuel
French Ltd (lyric) Copyright © 1996 by Nigel Bennetts (music)
All Rights Reserved

SPACE JUNK is fully protected under the copyright laws of the British Commonwealth, including Canada, the United States of America, and all other countries of the Copyright Union. All rights, including professional and amateur stage productions, recitation, lecturing, public reading, motion picture, radio broadcasting, television and the rights of translation into foreign languages are strictly reserved.

ISBN 978-0-573-05121-0

www.samuelfrench-london.co.uk

www.samuelfrench.com

For Amateur Production Enquiries

United Kingdom and World excluding North America

plays@SamuelFrench-London.co.uk

020 7255 4302/01

Each title is subject to availability from Samuel French,

depending upon country of performance.

CAUTION: Professional and amateur producers are hereby warned that *SPACE JUNK* is subject to a licensing fee. Publication of this play does not imply availability for performance. Both amateurs and professionals considering a production are strongly advised to apply to the appropriate agent before starting rehearsals, advertising, or booking a theatre. A licensing fee must be paid whether the title is presented for charity or gain and whether or not admission is charged.

The professional rights in this play are controlled by Samuel French Ltd, 52 Fitzroy Street, London, W1T 5JR.

No one shall make any changes in this title for the purpose of production. No part of this book may be reproduced, stored in a retrieval system, or transmitted in any form, by any means, now known or yet to be invented, including mechanical, electronic, photocopying, recording, videotaping, or otherwise, without the prior written permission of the publisher. No one shall upload this title, or part of this title, to any social media websites.

The right of Les Ellison to be identified as author of this work has been asserted by him in accordance with Section 77 of the Copyright, Designs and Patents Act 1988

CHARACTERS

Dumpster, an idealistic young rat
Uncle Binlid, Dumpster's down-to-earth uncle
Hamilton, an escaped hamster
Volga Ratskaya, a Russian space-castaway laboratory rat
Admiral Horatio Rodent, a sea-faring rat
Mr Hardy Bilge, the Admiral's very competent first mate
4 Sea-rats, the Admiral's crew (non speaking)
The Lord Vermin, tyrannic ruler of rats
Trash, Vermin's sycophantic valet
4 Guard-rats, Vermin's soldiers (non speaking)

The action of the play takes place in a city park and in outer space

Time: the present

PRODUCTION NOTES

The characters first appeared in the play *Utter Garbage*. *Space Junk* continues their adventures in the city park reclaimed from the rubbish dump. It is not necessary to have seen or performed *Utter Garbage* to make sense of, and enjoy, *Space Junk*.

The sexes of the characters, and the numbers of sea-rats and rat-guards, should be adapted to suit the available or desired cast. Extra material such as songs or dances may be introduced if desired, for example dancing starlets to cover rearrangements of the star-ship or in Binlid's dreams.

Volga is Russian and sometimes utters phrases in Russian. These are transcribed in an easy-to-follow phonetic notation, with the stress in the words indicated by underline.

The technical requirements are fairly simple. There are no curtains or back scene other than a black backdrop or gauze. Basic stage lighting would enhance the production. Cues for such are included in the script as are some simple sound effects. The sound effects are available from various sources including *BBC Essential Sound Effects (BBCCD 792)*. If the theatre is big enough, a smoke machine may add to the rocket take-off and space station break-up scenes.

The set props for the gardeners' corner are few and simple. They should be on the scale of the rat characters. The space and space station scenes require only a bare stage.

The star-ship is built from bits of oversized rubbish. A little imagination will go a long way. The main body of the star-ship can be a half section through a drinks can. This can be turned around to show its inside as required. A couple of triangular wafers for wings, and an ice cream cone for its nose cone, will finish the effect. Inverting them will provide a means of showing that the star-ship is upside down after its crash on to the space station.

The stars for the final effect can be simply made from white Christmas tree lights strung behind the black gauze and, if possible, everywhere else.

The music for the songs is included and the words are inserted in the text of the play. The tune for the Russian national anthem can be found in most multimedia encyclopaedias, and Tchaikovsky's *1812* is also easily found on recordings.

Music Credits:

The Wonder of It All, Volga's Song, Re-Entry Song : music and lyrics by Cheryl Lowery and Kirsty Body. *Space Junk Song*: lyrics by Les Ellison, music by Nigel Bennetts

SPACE JUNK

A Programme Note:

Since the world's first satellite began its orbit on 4th October 1957, there has been one new launch into space, on average, every three days. Over 7000 pieces of satellite and rocket, greater than 10cm in size, are now whizzing around the earth at 27,000 kilometres an hour. Below 10cm in size there are too many pieces to count. In 1983 a speck of paint just 0.2mm across from an old rocket, hit and cracked the window of a space ship. The outer-most layer of our planet is being cluttered with rubbish that may one day prevent us from reaching out to the stars. This rubbish is called Space Junk.

"Where there is no vision, the people perish."
Proverbs 29:18

For Haslingfield Young Little Theatre

ACT I

The gardener's corner of a city park recently reclaimed from a rubbish dump

There are one or two outsized plant pots and other gardening paraphernalia. Prominent is a sign saying "City Free Park" and another reminding visitors to "please take their litter home"

The stage is darkened

Binlid lies, peacefully sleeping, in a seed tray c. An oversized alarm clock stands close beside him. He is lit by a single blue light directly overhead

Binlid snores loudly. A clock ticks. This sound is joined by the ticking of another ... and another ... and another. The purpose is to build up the impression of a surrealistic nightmare but without terrifying the younger members of the audience. Suddenly an alarm clock rings loudly ... then another ... and others of different types. Even, perhaps, the chimes of Big Ben

Vermin, Trash and the Guard-rats move in from the gloom toward the seed tray. The Guard-rats are armed with pointed weapons such as oversize cocktail sticks, pencils or cutlery

Binlid's arm appears over the side of the tray as he gropes for the clock. Trash picks up the clock and throws it off the stage. There is a crash offstage, then silence

Binlid *(from within the tray)* Thank you. (*He yawns, turns over, and sleeps on*)
Vermin Uncle Binlid...

Trash and the Guard-rats whisper "Uncle Binlid" to effect a multiple echo

Uncle Binlid...

Trash and the Guard-rats echo Vermin's words as before

Wakey, wakey, Uncle Binlid.

"Wakey-wakey" is echoed, but now it sounds sinister and threatening

It's morning.

"Morning-morning" is echoed

(*Loudly*) Get up!

Trash and the Guard-rats loudly repeat "get up, get up" and tip Binlid out of his bed

Binlid (*tumbling from his bed and toward* DS) Aaaah!

Vermin stands on Binlid's upturned seed tray. He is lit by a red light from overhead

Vermin Uncle Binlid.
Binlid (*cowering* DS) V... V... Vermin?
Trash The Lord Vermin to you, Binlid. The Ruler of Refuse, Defender of Dumps and Guardian of Garbage. Stand and salute your Lord and Master.

Trash and the Guard-rats salute Vermin by cupping their hands to their heads, like rat's ears, and saying "Eek-Eek. Eek-Eek."

(*To the audience*) And you can show some respect and all. Come on, on your feet.

Guard-rats come DS and make the audience stand

Now, with me. Salute the Lord Vermin like this— (*he cups his hands to his head like rat's ears and leads the audience*) and say "Eek-Eek. Eek-Eek".
Binlid (*getting to his feet; to the audience*) No. Stop it. Don't salute him, he's evil and wicked and not at all nice.
Vermin Seize him!

Guard-rats seize Binlid

Inciting rebellion is a very serious crime for a ... garbage rat.
Binlid I'm not a garbage rat. And you ain't my ruler. I'm a free animal, see. Look, "City Free Park". The sign says so.
Vermin Reading, Binlid? Well, well... You have made progress. As I remember, you couldn't even count last time we met.

Act I

Binlid Yeah, well, I can now. And I can read that one as well. I'll read it for you if you like. It says "Take your litter home". And that's why there ain't no garbage here.
Vermin Ha! People never take their litter home. They can't be bothered.
Binlid Maybe not *growed-up* people. But *child*-people, now they's different, they is.
Vermin (*contemptuously*) Child-people.
Binlid Yeah, young ones. Look. (*To the audience*) Loads of 'em. (*He waves to the audience*)
Vermin I know what child-people are.
Binlid And look at this. (*He pulls free of the guards and goes* DS) See? Hardly any sweet papers on the floor at all. Mind you, we haven't got to the interval yet. Things are changing 'round here, see. Growed-up people are still a bit messy. That's why we still have bins. But the young ones, they always take their litter home.
Trash Oh, very good. Young ones—litter. Litter—young ones. Very funny. (*He giggles*)
Vermin Do shut up, Trash.
Trash (*recovering himself*) Sorry, your Ratship. (*He gives one last stifled giggle*)
Binlid It's a new world, Vermin...
Vermin Now where have I heard that before?
Binlid And it's all down to the child-people.
Vermin Hmm. Maybe I should do a little ... tidying up myself.
Binlid That's the spirit! You could start with...
Vermin I could start with you! (*He takes a weapon from a Guard-rat*) One less rebellious rat would make the world a much tidier place. Or at least it would make my world a tidier place. Which is ... (*he stabs at Binlid*) of course ... the same ... thing.
Binlid You can't mess up the whole world just to suit you, Vermin.
Vermin Oh, I can, Binlid, I can. And to prove it I'm going to start by messing up *your* world. Very ... very ... thoroughly. Guards!

The Guard-rats drive Binlid into a corner with their weapons. They are poised to finish him

Binlid Here... You can't do this. It's a Free Park this is... No, please... Aaaah!

Black-out

Binlid's cries merge into those of Dumpster

Dumpster Aaaah!

When the Lights come up, Vermin and company have gone. Binlid is lying on the floor. Dumpster, with a few twigs and leaves stuck in his clothes is sitting on him

Binlid Get off me, you villains! Get off me, get off me, get off me...

Dumpster looks around, puzzled, then suddenly realizes that the shouts are coming from underneath him

Dumpster Uncle Binlid, Uncle Binlid. Wake up, Uncle Binlid, it's me. It's Dumpster.
Binlid What the... *(He calms down)* Dumpster. What are you doing here?
Dumpster I fell on top of you. I think you were dreaming again.
Binlid Dreaming? It was more like a nightmare. *(He gets up and looks for his vanished tormentors)* And the Lord Vermin was in it. And Trash. And the Guard-rats tried to... And they were going to... I mean I thought they was... I mean...
Dumpster It's your imagination, that's all. Sometimes it doesn't turn off when you go to sleep.
Binlid It was so real. *(To himself)* Where's my alarm clock?
Dumpster Vermin's gone, Uncle Binlid. Remember? Captain Rodent and the sea-rats chased him away. He doesn't rule us any more. We're free animals. We can do anything we please.

Hamilton enters, wearing a night cap and a dressing-gown over her tracksuit

Hamilton Except sleep, *(she yawns)* ...apparently.
Dumpster Morning, Hamilton. You're up early.
Hamilton Up early? How many times do I have to remind you. Hamsters are nocturnal animals. I'm not up early, I'm up late. I was just settling down to a good day's sleep when all this crashing and banging and shouting woke me up. It's not right so it isn't. *(She gets herself comfortable on Binlid's upturned bed)*
Dumpster Sorry, Hamilton. Uncle Binlid's been dreaming again.
Hamilton I should be so lucky. *(She yawns and settles down to sleep)*
Dumpster He was dreaming about Vermin.
Binlid He was going to do me in. Till Dumpster fell on me and woke me up.
Hamilton You have my deepest sympathy.
Binlid Hang on a minute. Where was you when you fell on me, young Dumpster?
Dumpster On top of you, of course.
Hamilton Oh, very funny.

Act I

Binlid No. Just before that. Where did you fall from?
Dumpster The big oak tree. I *was* trying to get down, honest.
Binlid You shouldn't have been up there in the first place. We're rats, not squirrels. We got no business climbing trees.
Dumpster I was looking at the stars. (*He moves* DS *and looks upwards*)
Binlid You can see them perfectly well from down here.
Dumpster I wanted to see them close up. They're so bright, Uncle Binlid, and they twinkle. And not all the same colour. And some of them move. Really quickly. They shoot across the sky... Whoosh! And leave a little trail of light. Then it just fades away like it was never there... Where do the shooting stars go?
Binlid Dunno. (*He shakes his head*) That kind of thing's way over my head.
Dumpster And the stars make patterns. If you join them up they make pictures. There's a bear and a lion and a swan and all sorts of things.
Binlid But there's no rat, is there?
Dumpster Can't see one.
Binlid Well, there you are then. If you can't see a rat in the stars then they're nothing to do with us.
Hamilton (*still trying to sleep*) I know a few rats who'll see stars if they don't be quiet.
Dumpster I'm going up there one day. I'm going to the stars... And the stars beyond the stars. And the stars beyond the stars beyond the stars. And the stars beyond the stars beyond the stars beyond the...

Hamilton rises, takes her night cap and pulls it down with such force over Dumpster's head, to silence him, that Dumpster is pushed to the floor. Satisfied, Hamilton returns to bed

(*Pulling off the night cap*) I'm going to reach the stars. I am. I am.
Rodent (*off; shouting*) Hard a' starboard, Mr Bilge. Steady as she goes.
Hamilton Oh, no. Please, not them, please! (*She buries herself in her bed clothes*)

Sea-shanty music accompanies the Sea-rats, lead by Bilge, as they guide in a boat clearly made from a sardine tin. In the boat sits Rodent shouting instructions through a megaphone. Binlid's smashed alarm clock is also in the boat

Rodent (*ad lib as necessary*) Half ahead both, Mr Bilge... Prepare to drop anchor.
Bilge Half ahead both, sir. Anchor ready.
Rodent Very good, Mr Bilge. Drop anchor.
Bilge Aye, aye, sir.

The Sea-rats steer the sardine tin to rest DC. *Bilge stands the Sea-rats to attention at one side. Rodent steps out of his vessel to the enthusiastic greetings of Dumpster. Sea-rats then set to securing the sardine tin, unloading the alarm clock etc.*

Dumpster Captain Rodent! Mr Bilge!
Rodent Ship ahoy, young fella me rat. Long time no see, what?
Dumpster What are you doing here?
Rodent Well, we were just circumnavigating the jolly old duck pond over there, when this alarm clock sort of thing hit us amidships.
Binlid (*puzzled*) But ... that's *my* alarm clock.
Rodent Yes. Hope you're not going to make a habit of this sort of thing.

Rodent returns the clock to a clearly confused Binlid

Thought we'd better return it. Couldn't have you over-sleeping.
Hamilton Not much chance of that around here. (*She gives up her attempts to sleep, takes off her dressing-gown and starts doing a few exercises*)
Rodent I say, Mr Bilge. It's that keep-fit chap. Met her in a garden once. No tail.
Hamilton (*examining her stubby tail*) Yes, I have.
Rodent What's her name, now? Sorry, got a memory like an erm ... thing. Full of holes. Wash vegetables in 'em.
Bilge Colander, sir.
Rodent Don't think so, Mr Bilge. Go all soggy. Ink would run. Wouldn't know what month it was. Honestly, for a clever chap you can be a bit short on the old common sense.
Bilge (*resignedly*) Sir.
Dumpster Strainer! A Strainer.
Rodent There you are. Jolly nice to meet you again, Ms A. Strainer.
Hamilton The name's Hamilton.
Rodent Course it is. Yes. Shame about the tail, though. Sporting injury, was it?
Hamilton (*affronted*) This is all the tail I'm supposed to have.
Bilge (*trying to explain*) Sir, Hamilton was a pet, sir. A caged animal. Escaped from the garden with young Dumpster. Lives here now. The City Park. Where the rubbish dump used to be, sir. Before it got recycled?
Rodent I'm not a thickee rat, Mr Bilge. So. Lost the old tail in a daring escape, then?

Others on stage hang their heads in despair

Hamilton I AM A HAMSTER!

Act I

Rodent (*taking Bilge aside*) Really got to get your facts right, Mr Bilge. Now we've got bit of diplomatic incident here.
Bilge You don't say, sir.
Rodent You learn to notice these things when you're an admiral. I'll use a bit of tact and we just might get away with it.

Behind Rodent, Dumpster and Binlid are restraining Hamilton who is intent on strangling him

Sensitivity, you see. That's the thing when dealing with land animals. Now. Let's see if I can't patch things up.
Bilge Sir, rather than patch things up. May I suggest we start again.
Rodent Good idea. Pretend it never happened.
Bilge Sir...

Binlid is giving Hamilton a stiff talking to and Dumpster is trying to calm things down

Rodent Right. Formal introductions. When all else fails, stand on protocol, that's what I always say. 'Tention, all.

Bilge and Sea-rats stand to attention

Admiral Horatio Rodent, that's me. Mr Hardy Bilge, first mate. And the jolly old Sea-rats, crew of the Good Ship erm... (*He turns to read the side of the boat*) Sardines in Tomato Sauce.
Bilge (*whispering*) New World, sir. Named by young Dumpster. Remember?
Rodent 'Course I remember, Mr Bilge. I am an admiral, you know.
Binlid So it's Admiral now, is it?
Rodent (*showing off the gold braid on his uniform*) Spot of promotion.
Binlid Reward for dealing with the Lord Vermin, I expect.
Rodent No. Actually got a medal for that. Whole crew got decorated.

Sea-rats proudly display their medals

Order of the Valorous Whisker. Got the old Admiral bit for services to navigation. When we sailed into that rubbish dump of yours, and then into erm...
All Hamilton.
Rodent That's right, her garden, rather opened up a world *we'd* never even imagined.
Dumpster (*dreamily*) A world we'd never *imagined*... (*He wanders* DC *gazing up into the sky*)

Rodent Sailed off the jolly old map, so we did. Isn't that right, Mr Bilge?
Bilge Very true, sir. Had to redraw every map and chart in the fleet.
Rodent So here we are. On a brand new mission. See what else is off the edge of the map. "To boldly go where no jolly old rat's gone before." Sort of a... *Rat's Trek*, I suppose.
Binlid But still sailing around in *my* sardine tin.
Rodent Ah. The jolly old boat. It's amazing what a bit of this erm...
Bilge Recycling, sir.
Rodent Recycling can do. Finds a use for practically everything, you know.
Binlid It already had a use. It was my bed until you sailed off in it. And without asking.
Hamilton Uncle Binlid.

Hamilton draws Binlid's attention to Dumpster standing dreamily DS

Binlid Oh, no. Not again. I've seen him like this before. It always brings trouble.
Dumpster (*dreamily*) To boldly go where no rat has gone before.

Hamilton moves to Dumpster, intending to gently bring him down to earth. They engage in silent conversation. As Dumpster points out the wonders and marvels of the heavens, it becomes clear that Hamilton is being won over by Dumpster's idealistic enthusiasm

Binlid Yes. Well, I think it's time you were trekking off now.

Binlid tries to usher Rodent and his crew away from Dumpster and off the stage

Rodent But we've only just arrived.
Binlid Oh, no. I think you've been here far too long already.
Rodent Rather fancied giving the old Sea-rats a spot of shore leave.

Sea-rats eagerly nod their approval of this intention

Binlid No, no. You don't want to do that. Wouldn't do them any good at all. Best get 'em back to sea where they're happy. Bye now. Safe journey.
Rodent Now steady on. (*He resists*) This is jolly ungrateful. After all, we did help you sort out that Vermin chap.
Binlid Help us? You nearly got us all killed. Putting ideas into young Dumpster's head. You and all this New World nonsense. (*He kicks the sardine tin boat*)
Bilge With respect, sir. I rather think the idea was Dumpster's own doing.

I don't think we can claim the credit for that. Though ... we may have helped him along a bit.

The argument has attracted Dumpster's attention

Binlid Exactly. You took him off in that boat and showed him gardens and flowers and trees. Really upset him that did. Until you come along we were perfectly happy where we were. Living in our lives in——

Dumpster Utter garbage. We were up to our whiskers in stinking rubbish. And we only *thought* we were happy 'cos we didn't *know* what happy really was.

Binlid (*mellowing*) Yes. All right, I'm sorry. Things *was* bad before. But they're fine now, aren't they? Vermin's gone and so has all the rubbish. Look, I know what you're thinking. And it's not worth it. Think of what you might loose.

Dumpster But think of what we might find.

Rodent There. Hear that, you Sea-rats? (*He moves to put his arm around Dumpster's shoulders*) That's the kind of talk I like to hear. What's he on about, Mr Bilge?

Bilge Not quite sure, sir.

Dumpster Are there any maps of ... Up There?

Binlid Oh, no. Not that. Please not that.

Bilge Well, there's the Star Charts. We use them to find our way at night.

Rodent Jolly useful. Don't work too well in a sewer for some reason. Don't know why.

Dumpster So if your mission is to go *beyond* the maps and charts...

Binlid Here it comes.

Dumpster Then you have to go ... Up There.

Binlid Told you so.

Bilge Well. That *would* seem to be within the remit of our orders. Sir?

Rodent (*checking his orders*) Absolutely, Mr Bilge. "To boldly go..." and all that. Boldly. No doubt about it. Make the ship ready, Mr Bilge. Set a course for ... that way. (*He points up*)

Bilge Not sure the old ship's up to boldly going anywhere, sir. Not since the direct hit from that alarm clock. Hardly up to navigating the sewers, never mind the stars.

Binlid Really? (*He hides his relief*) Oh, dear. S'pose we'll just have to stay at home after all. What a terrible shame. Never mind, I'll put the kettle on.

Dumpster What you *need* is a starship.

Binlid What *you* need is a...

Rodent Difficult thing to come by in a city park, I shouldn't wonder.

Hamilton Couldn't we ... well, couldn't we just make one?

Binlid Not you as well.

Hamilton The good ship *New World*'s made out of recycled rubbish.
Binlid It was made out of my bed!
Hamilton So a starship can't be much more difficult.
Binlid Oh, it is. Much more difficult. Almost impossible. And anyway, there's no rubbish in a city park. See? Perfectly clean and tidy. So that's, err, what, [nine] teas? Milk and sugar?
Dumpster There is rubbish. It's in the rubbish bins. All we have to do is go and get it.
Rodent Jolly good. Mr Bilge. Organise the Sea-rats into shore parties. See the youngsters get everything they need to build a starship. I'll stay here and sort of supervise things.
Bilge Yes, sir. Right away, sir.

Bilge sends two of the Sea-rats off R *and the other two off* L. *They return with outsized pieces of rubbish*

The Lights dim US. *Bilge, Dumpster and Hamilton assemble the pieces into the rocket ship* US. *Binlid moves* DS *and gloomily sits with his head in his hands. Rodent joins him*

Rodent Cheer up, there. Things could be worse, you know.
Binlid That's just what a rat says just before things *get* worse. Usually much worse.
Rodent Steady on. Got to admire a youngster's sense of adventure.
Binlid Yes. But you're not responsible for him, are you? You ain't his guardian.
Rodent Doesn't mean I don't care for the little fella. And that, erm ... hamster chap.
Binlid Well, you've got a funny way of showing it. "Boldly going where a rat's never gone before".
Rodent Youngsters are *natural* adventurers. Born to it, they are. It's in their whiskers.
Binlid Ain't no excuse for letting them get themselves into trouble. It's a growed-rat's job to keep a youngster's paws on the ground. Not go shooting them off to the stars.
Rodent At ease, Uncle Binlid. You must have been a nipper once yourself. Had dreams of your own, eh? Never wanted to push the jolly old boat out a bit?
Binlid No! Well... Yes. Once. (*Distantly*) Quite fancied the Rat Navy, actually. Had an offer, too. Midshipman on *The Far Horizon*. But then there was Vermin. And that business with Dumpster's mum and dad ... and the cat. Poor young nipper. (*He snaps back*) So I haven't time for dreams, see. I've got responsibilities. I've got a nephew to look after.

Rodent Well, deepest sympathies and all that. But a rat's got to find his *own* place in the world.
Binlid Yeah, that's right. *In* the world. In *this* world. Not in some other world. Not up there where no rat's boldly gone. Maybe no rat's boldly *gone* there because no rat's supposed to *be* there.
Rodent Or maybe it's because no rat's been bold enough to go.

Behind them, the assembly of the starship is nearing completion. The Lights come up US

Bilge Starship ready for your inspection, sir.
Rodent Jolly good, Mr Bilge. Have the Sea-rats fall in and we'll make a proper job of it.

Bilge stands the Sea-rats to attention. Dumpster and Hamilton are not visible. Binlid looks on as Rodent inspects the starship

Jolly good... Jolly good, indeed... A fine-looking ship, Mr Bilge. A fine-looking ship, indeed... My compliments to the crew.
Bilge Thank you, sir.
Rodent Quite exciting, don't you think; sharp end to the stars and all that.
Bilge Quite, sir.
Rodent Where's young Dumpster and, erm ... the hamster chap?

A small door opens in the starship and Dumpster and Hamilton enter through it on to the stage. They wear silvery space suits, apparently made from sweet wrappers or tin foil

Binlid You ain't still serious about this?
Dumpster We've got to, Uncle Binlid. We've just got to.
Rodent Right. Better give her a name then. *The New World Two*, I suppose.
Dumpster No, the world's out there on the *outside*. This is about something on the *inside*.
Hamilton Yes. A sort of feeling. Makes you want to reach out and touch the stars.
Binlid (*resignedly*) Spirit. That's what it is. It's called the spirit.
Dumpster (*in wonder*) The *New Spirit*.

Murmurs of approval and excitement go around the Sea-rats

Rodent I name this ship: The *New Spirit*.
All except Binlid The *New Spirit*!
Rodent Right. All aboard, Mr Bilge. Hoist the mainsail and make ready to weigh anchor.

Bilge Don't think you can actually *sail* a starship, sir.

Rodent 'Course not, Mr Bilge. Got a bit carried away there. Break out the oars, you Sea-rats. I want [two] on this side with Mr Bilge and another [two] on this side with me.

Bilge Sir, I think the usual method is to burn hydrogen and oxygen in a rocket motor. It's a question of generating sufficient thrust to escape the Earth's gravity.

Hamilton Hadn't thought of that.

Rodent Rocket motor, eh?

Bilge Yes, sir.

Rodent Suppose you can't make one out of ... paper cups and drinking straws?

Bilge No, sir.

There is a general air of disappointment

Rodent Well. Looks like we're back to mapping the sewers, Mr Bilge. Better get the Sea-rats fed and we'll be on our way.

Bilge Yes, sir.

Binlid There's some cheese sandwiches in the bin by the car park. I saw them there last night. I was going to have them for my tea, but ... oh, well.

Bilge Very kind, Mr Binlid. Sea-rats! Foraging party ... with me. Left, right, left...

Bilge and the Sea-rats leave

Dumpster and Hamilton look dejectedly at the static starship

Rodent (*to Binlid*) Well. Looks like you're going to keep your feet on the ground after all.

Binlid Yeh. Funny though, I'm almost sorry it didn't work. Yeh. Sorry, Dumpster. Really I am.

Dumpster That's all right. You can't expect *all* your dreams to come true. Not all at once anyway.

Hamilton And we *might* wake up one day and find someone's dumped a rocket motor in a litter bin. You never know.

Dumpster No. You never know.

Binlid Come on you two. No use sitting around. Better get all this stuff back in the bins. Gardener'll think his park's overrun with garbage rats.

Dumpster (*removing his silvery suit*) Don't suppose I'll be needing this.

Hamilton (*likewise*) I was beginning to feel like a chocolate biscuit anyway.

Binlid, Dumpster and Hamilton start to dismantle the starship

Act I

Bilge and the Sea-rats enter, carrying lumps of clearly very ripe cheese

Bilge You were right about the cheese there, Mr Binlid. Just the sort of thing to put a chap back on his feet. (*He gives his cheese to Rodent*)
Rodent Mmm. (*He smells the cheese approvingly and offers a lump to Hamilton*)
Hamilton Phwor!! (*She recoils at the smell of the cheese and falls flat on her back*)
Binlid It's just the sort of thing put a chap flat on his back!
Rodent Oh. Thought it was quite pleasant myself. (*He offers his cheese to Dumpster*)
Dumpster Phwor!! (*He also recoils at the smell and falls flat on his back*)
Bilge Well done, sir! I think you've just solved our rocket problem.
Rodent I have? Well. Jolly well done me, eh? How's that then, Mr Bilge?
Bilge Newton's Third Law of Motion, sir: "For every action there is an equal and opposite reaction."
Rodent Gosh, I love science, Mr Bilge. Just wish I had the faintest idea what it was all about.
Bilge Sir. If we can present enough cheese to enough noses then the reaction should be big enough to blast the starship into space.
Rodent Certainly got enough cheese, Mr Bilge. Dashed if I know where to find enough noses.
Dumpster The child-people!
Hamilton Yes. The child-people. (*To the audience*) You'll help us, won't you?

Dumpster and Hamilton move DS and encourage a positive response

Dumpster Of course they will.
Hamilton When we hold up the cheese, you take a deep breath and go... *Phwor!!*
Bilge I'm afraid it needs to be a co-ordinated "Phwor". If they don't … "Phwor" exactly all together, then it won't work. May even end in disaster.
Hamilton Oh, dear…
Rodent Well. Sounds like a military operation to me. Sea-rats! Line abreast. Dress by the centre. Cheeses … at the ready.

Sea-rats move DS and dress their line, holding their cheeses in cupped hands

Bilge Now we need a signal.
Rodent What, like a flag or something?
Binlid I don't know… (*He reluctantly gets involved*) Look. If you're going to do something, do it properly. To get it exactly together, you got to have a countdown. It's just like, counting, but *backwards*.

Rodent As you wish. Sea-rats. About ... face!

The Sea-rats smartly about-face

Bilge Sir. Mr Binlid means *counting* backwards. In descending order of magnitude.
Rodent Ah. Sea-rats ... as you were.

Sea-rats turn about to face the audience

Binlid (*to the audience*) Right, we're going to count from five down to one. Like this... "Five ... four ... three ... two ... one." All right? Good, let's have a practice.

Dumpster, Hamilton, Bilge and Rodent join in to practice the countdown with the audience

Then after "one", Admiral Rodent's going to shout "Present Cheese". All the Sea-rats are going to present their smelly cheese to your noses and you're going to take a deep breath. Like this... (*He breathes in, deeply*) Right, let's practice that far. But no cheese just yet, if you don't mind.
All Five ... four ... three ... two ... one...
Rodent Present cheese.

No cheese is presented in this practice run

Binlid Deep breath!

All on stage breathe in deeply and hold it

There. What d'you think? (*He turns to Bilge and the others*) I mean, we could count down from ten if you like, but... Sorry ... what's that?

Dumpster, Hamilton and Bilge, with inflated chests and cheeks, point frantically at the audience to remind Binlid that he hasn't told them to breathe out

Oh... Breathe out! Breathe out! Breathe out! Sorry about that, forgot you were holding your breath. Right. This time, with the smelly cheese. So it's "Five ... four ... three ... two ... one... Present cheese. Deep breath. And a big... Phwor!!" Ready? Right. This one's for real... (*He leads the audience*)
All Five ... four ... three ... two ... one...

Act I

Rodent Present cheese!

Sea-rats hold their cheese at arm's length to the audience

Binlid Deep breath… And…
All with the audience Phwor!!

All on stage turn to look at the starship. It hasn't moved, hopefully

Bilge Needs a lot more reaction, I'm afraid, Mr Binlid.
Binlid Right. Come on, child-people. You can do better than that. Ready? (*He leads the audience, this time with more urgency*)
All Five… Four… Three… Two… One…
Rodent Present cheese!

Sea-rats stretch their cheese-arms further into the audience

Binlid Deep breath… And…
All with the audience Phwor!!

There is the sound of a rocket motor and a gently pulsating light

Bilge It's working! One more really good "Phwor" should do it.
Binlid This is it, child-people. This has got to come from deep down inside. Ready? Right. For the *New Spirit*! (*He leads the audience, with extreme urgency*)
All FIVE … FOUR … THREE … TWO … ONE…!
Rodent PRESENT CHEESE!!

Sea-rats wave their cheese frantically at the audience

Binlid Deep breath… And…
All with the audience PHWORRRRR!!!

The rocket motor grows steadily louder. The pulsating light gets stronger

Dumpster It's working! It's working! Uncle Binlid, you did it.
Binlid Don't blame me. It was the child-people, they did it.
Dumpster Thank you, child-people. Don't go away, we might need you again.
Rodent Magnificent sight, Mr Bilge. Our ship. On its way to the stars.
Bilge May I suggest we get aboard, sir? Before it goes to the stars without us.
Rodent Right. Yes. Well… (*Through his megaphone*) All aboard the *Skylark*!

Dumpster The *New Spirit*! (*He climbs through the door of the starship*)
Rodent *New Spirit*. Yes. What ever happened to *real* ship's names. (*He follows Dumpster*)
Hamilton Looks like I'm going to be a chocolate biscuit after all. (*She picks up the silvery suits and follows into the starship*)
Bilge Come on there, Sea-rats. Better bring along that cheese, too. Goodness knows when we'll get fed again.

Sea-rats and Bilge follow into the starship

Binlid Somehow, I just know I'm going to regret this. (*He follows last*)

The rocket motor reaches its full volume

Black-out

In the darkness, the starship is reversed to show its inside to the audience. On Lights up, only the starship interior is lit against a black stage. Sitting facing the audience is Bilge at some rudimentary controls made from the broken alarm clock. Dumpster and Hamilton sit, wide-eyed, beside him. The Sea-rats sit on the floor in front. Binlid and Rodent stand behind looking at a map. The rocket noise grows quieter and stops. There is silence. Dumpster and Hamilton wander DS. A weak light picks them out as they speak. They appear awestruck by the sheer magnitude and blackness of space

Dumpster Where have the clouds gone? And the sky.
Hamilton They're behind us. We're in space.
Dumpster Look at the stars. And the moon. They're so bright.
Hamilton There's no pollution up here. At least not yet.

There is a rushing noise. It gets cyclically louder and quieter as a bright spotlight sweeps around and around the stage and auditorium. Dumpster and Hamilton watch it, fascinated

Dumpster What was that?
Hamilton I think it was a comic. Or maybe a metronome, or an, erm ... asterisk.
Dumpster You are clever, Hamilton.
Hamilton I try to keep up. Healthy body, healthy mind, and all that.
Dumpster And there's the Earth. Isn't it beautiful?
Hamilton Isn't it small? I'd be afraid it might get broken hanging around up here.

Act I

Song 1: The Wonder Of It All

Dumpster (*singing*) The wonder of it all.
        The stars so high above me.
        The magic of the skies
        The moon so clear and free.
        The planets silently spinning
        With shades of ev'ry hue.
Hamilton (*joining in*) I long to be there among them
        Exploring, me and you.
        There's galaxies and meteors
        Just waiting to be found.
        There's asteroids and shooting stars
        The heavenly bodies abound.

After singing, Hamilton and Dumpster sit on the edge of the stage watching the heavens. The stage lighting on them dims, and becomes concentrated on the inside of the starship US

Bilge Shall I set a course, sir?
Rodent S'pose we'd better, Mr Bilge.
Bilge Where to, sir?
Rodent To the edge of the map, I think. And a bit further.
Bilge Very good, sir. Any preferences as to which edge?
Rodent No. One edge is much the same as the other really. (*He turns the map over and over in a hopelessly puzzled sort of way*)
Bilge Perhaps that's just as well, sir.
Binlid Meaning what?
Bilge Newton's First Law. Nothing moves or stops or steers unless something makes it move or stop...
Binlid Or steer.
Bilge Precisely.
Binlid And we haven't got anything to steer with, have we?
Bilge (*uselessly turning the controls round and around*) Apparently not.
Binlid I knew something like this was going to happen. I'll go and see what else we're short of.

Binlid leaves through the door in the back of the starship

Rodent (*with the map rolled up into a telescope*) How many kilometre-thingies to the edge of the map, Mr Bilge?
Bilge I believe space distance is measured in *light-years*, sir.
Rodent I think I feel another spot of science coming on here, Mr Bilge.

Bilge Sir. Light travels at about three hundred thousand kilometres a second, sir. So a *light-year* is the distance travelled in one *year* at the *speed* of light.
Rodent Well. So how long to, erm ... that swirly thing over there.
Bilge That's a galaxy, sir. It's about two million light years away.
Rodent So. A bit of spare time for the odd game of I-Spy, then. (*He looks around at the obvious shortage of things to actually spy in the blackness of space*) Hmm...
Bilge The accepted practice is suspended animation, sir.
Rodent (*confidentially*) Aren't animated suspenders a bit saucy for a child-people's play?
Bilge Suspended animation, sir. It's a bit like hibernation.
Rodent Well, why didn't you say so, Mr Bilge? Could do with a spot of shut eye myself.

Sea-rats have begun to fall asleep against each other on the floor

So could the jolly old Sea-rats by the looks of them. Right, you chaps. Off to bed. Come on. You take first watch, Mr Bilge. We'll relieve you in ... erm...
Bilge (*resignedly*) A few million light-years, sir.
Rodent Yes. Righto. Erm... Well. Night-night, everyone.

Rodent and the Sea-rats leave through the door in the starship. Binlid enters the same way

Binlid Well, you'll be relieved to know that there's nothing.
Bilge Nothing missing?
Binlid No. There's nothing. Nothing at all. We're two hundred kilometres above the Earth in an empty tin with no steering, no brakes and no food. Still, things could be worse, I suppose.
Bilge That's the spirit!
Binlid No. That's sarcasm!

Dumpster and Hamilton come running back from the front of the stage

Dumpster Uncle Binlid, Uncle Binlid...
Binlid Don't panic, I'm sure we can...
Dumpster Look, the edge of the map. The edge of the star chart!
Binlid What?

All strain to peer into the darkness over the audience

Bilge It's a bit difficult to tell one shade of black from another... But I think he's right.

Act I

Binlid Blimey, I didn't expect it to look that solid.
Bilge Best prepare for a crash landing.

Bilge and Binlid set to clearing the interior fittings of the starship out through the door. (This is actually to make the next change easier.) Dumpster and Hamilton run DS to the audience

Dumpster This isn't going to be very pleasant. We could do with a bit of warning before we crash. Will you count us down? You will? Thanks.
Hamilton When we do this—(*he holds up five fingers*) we need you to count down (*he counts on his fingers*) "five ... four ... three ... two ... one..." then close your eyes tight and put your fingers in your ears. Will you do that? You are good, you know.

Dumpster and Hamilton run back to the starship interior. All prepare for the worst

Bilge Here it comes. Brace yourselves, everyone.
Hamilton Now!

Dumpster and Hamilton lead the audience in the countdown

All Five ... four ... three ... two ... one...

They put their fingers in their ears. There is a deafening and prolonged crash. Lights flash quickly and brightly. Then silence and Black-out. In the black-out, the starship is turned around to show its outside. The moveable parts are inverted and rearranged to make it appear nose down. The Lights come up on the upside-down, crashed starship. The stage is empty. There is no sign of life

CURTAIN

—An interval may be inserted here if required—
The stage may be left with the crashed starship in view

ACT II

The upside-down starship stands UC *on an otherwise empty stage*

The door falls open. After a few seconds Dumpster crawls out. He wanders DS, *looking around. Hamilton and Bilge emerge behind him. They are shaken and dishevelled but not seriously hurt*

Dumpster Where are we?
Bilge Don't rightly know, I'm afraid.
Dumpster Are we off the edge of the charts?
Bilge I wouldn't have thought so. We haven't been travelling for nearly long enough.
Dumpster Then where are they? (*He looks upward for the stars*)
Binlid (*emerging from the starship*) Still asleep.
Bilge Sorry?
Binlid The Admiral and Sea-rats. Suspended what's-it. Slept through the whole thing, they have. (*He notices the state of the starship*) Blimey, this is a mess.
Dumpster I mean the stars. Where are the stars? I can't see them.

Binlid examines the damaged starship. Hamilton and Bilge come DS *to join Dumpster. They also look around for the stars*

   See. There aren't any. We *must* have gone further than the stars.
Hamilton Well, if we have, we should be able to see them behind us.

Dumpster, Hamilton and Bilge turn to look US *behind them*

Black-out

Binlid Now what's going on?
Dumpster Well?
Hamilton No stars over here.
Bilge Nothing here either. Odd, really...

They turn back to face the audience. The Lights come up

   We should be able to see something.

Act II

Hamilton Maybe we just haven't got used to the dark yet.
Bilge Good thinking. Let's have another look.

They turn to look US *behind them*

Black-out

Unnoticed, Volga joins them. She wears a tattered silvery space-suit like a castaway

Binlid Will you stop doing that. I'm trying to work over here.
Hamilton It's no good. I still can't see any stars. How about you, Dumpster?
Dumpster It's like they've been blotted out. I don't like it, Mr Bilge. It's all so ... empty.
Bilge Cheer up, young fella. There'll be a good reason for it. There always is.

They turn back to face the audience. The Lights come up. Volga is next to Dumpster

Binlid Thank you. (*He turns*) Great rat's tails! Where did she come from!
Dumpster Who come from? (*He notices Volga with great surprise*) Ahh!
Volga (*equally surprised by Dumpster*) Ahh! (*She runs and hides behind the starship*)
Binlid (*moving* DS *to join the others*) Who was that?
Dumpster She frightened me out of my whiskers.
Hamilton I think you were a bit of a shock to her.
Bilge Well, whoever she is, she might be able to tell us where we are.
Binlid And maybe how to get back home. Where is she anyway?
Dumpster She went behind the starship.

Volga looks out timidly from behind the starship

Hamilton Poor thing's terrified.
Binlid Here, Dumpster. We'll hold back. You go and see if you can't make friends. Show her we mean no harm.

Binlid, Hamilton and Bilge move away. Dumpster approaches the starship and the frightened Volga. Dumpster raises his hand to wave. Volga ducks back down in fright

Dumpster Sorry. Sorry. I didn't mean to frighten you. We don't mean any harm. We're lost, that's all. We thought you might be able to tell us where we are.

Volga stays in view but doesn't respond

I don't think she understands.
Bilge Reach out your hand, young fella. Everyone understands that.

Dumpster tentatively offers his hand. Volga watches, then cautiously steps from her hiding place and warily takes Dumpster's hand. Their confidence in each other grows. Volga shakes Dumpster's hand vigorously then embraces him in a bear-hug, thumping him on the back

Volga Dubbrorpuzharluvvat! Dubbrorpuzharluvvat! [Welcome! Welcome!] I am a delight to meet you. (*She rushes around to the others, joyously shaking their hands and hugging them*) Dubbror puzharluvvat! Dubbror puzharluvvat! [Welcome! Welcome!]
Binlid Yes. And we are a...

Volga hugs him

(*Winded*) ...huh ... delight to meet you.
Volga I not meet other animal for too many years.
Dumpster You live here by yourself?
Volga For too long I live here. Too long. But now is over. Now you come take me home!
Binlid Erm... Yes. Actually we might have a little problem with that.
Volga Problem?
Bilge (*stepping in*) Perhaps you could tell us where we are.
Volga This People's Space Station "Pridstarveet sibbyeh" [Imagine]. I... (*She salutes*) Laboratory Animal First Class, Volga Ratskaya.

Volga sings the tune of the Russian national anthem. The others politely stand to attention and salute. Volga pauses for breath after each phrase. Dumpster takes each break as the end and tries to introduce himself only to have to snap back to attention as she starts again. Eventually she finishes

Dumpster I'm Dumpster. What are you doing here?
Volga Once I do space research. I run in maze. I choose this vay I choose that vay. I choose right: I get cheese. I not hungry: I choose wrong. Is simple. But now... I do nothing. Space station is finish. They leave me here. Alone. Five hundred kilometres in space. I just go round and round Earth. Round and round and round at thirty thousand kilometres in hour.
Hamilton I had a wheel like that once. Someone oiled the axle. I just couldn't stop it.

Act II

Song 2: Volga's Song

Volga (*singing*) When I was being a young rat, I lived myself to please.
But then I came to spaceship the people they did seize me
To run around in mazes and seek the bits of cheese.
Then they all did leave me.
Won't you help me please?

Round and round at thirty thousand kilometre-hour I go.
Round and round at thirty thousand kilometre-hour I go.
Round and round and round and round
And round and round and round for ever.

For many years I live here, I stay here on my own.
With no-one that I can talk to, not even mobile phone.
Five hundred kilometres above the Earth roam
So lonely I become, please,
Won't you take me home?

Hamilton (*joining in*) Round and round at thirty thousand kilometre-hour we go.
Round and round at thirty thousand kilometre-hour we go.
Round and round and round and round
And round and round and round for ever.

Volga Nobody care about me. Nobody care about space station. (*She breaks down*) Just I go round and round and round and...

Hamilton I know, I know... (*Sympathetically*) I'm Hamilton. I'm a hamster. I know all about going round and round and round. (*She puts her arm around Volga*)

Bilge A space station. We're on a derelict space station.

Binlid Well, I knew it wasn't Kansas.

Volga But now vee take off. You have spacecraft, yes? You have Soyuz? Apollo? No, no. You have ... how you say... Space Shuttle, yes?

Binlid Erm... (*He looks at the heap that constitutes their starship*) No. We have the erm ... *New Spirit*.

Volga *New Spirit*! Is good name. Is very good name for spacecraft. Name to reach stars!

Binlid Erm ... that was the *general* idea, yes.

Volga Now it take heroes back to homes! Vhere is spacecraft? Over here, yes? Behind garbage? (*She disappears behind the starship to search for her idea of a spacecraft*)

Binlid Actually, the garbage *is* the spacecraft.

Silence. Volga slowly reappears from behind the starship. She surveys the heap of rubbish

Volga Is joke, yes?

Others shake their heads apologetically

Dumpster Sorry.
Volga Is just more rubbish to go round and round. No matter. Is ... how you say ... too good to be being true anyvay.
Binlid I know it's not much to look at...
Volga Is not so bad. I have friends stay here vith me now. (*She puts her arms around the shoulders of the nearest animals*)
Binlid Here. Now you just hold on a minute. We ain't staying here...
Dumpster *We're* going to the stars ... wherever they are.
Binlid We're *going* home.
Bilge We're not going *anywhere* if we don't get the *New Spirit* shipshape again.
Volga Is nothing here. Is just rubbish and garbage now.
Binlid Yeah. Well, we're pretty good with rubbish and garbage. There's got to be something here we can recycle, hasn't there?
Bilge Very true, sir. We'll form search parties. Hamilton and Volga come with me, Dumpster and———
Binlid Better if the four of you stay together. Then if one gets into trouble two can stay to help and one come and fetch me. Anyway, Volga's the only one who knows her way around this place. I'll wait here until the Admiral and his crew wake up. Tell 'em what's going on.
Bilge Sound leadership, Uncle Binlid, sir. Rat Navy could use an animal like you.
Binlid No thanks, I've seen what it takes to make Admiral.
Bilge Sir. Right. Volga, you lead. Then Dumpster, Hamilton, and I'll bring up the rear. And remember, never loose sight of the tail in front. Back within the hour, sir.
Binlid On your way, Mr Bilge. Just you take care, you youngsters...

Bilge leads Hamilton, Dumpster and Volga off

(*Shouting after them*) And mind you do as you're told.
Dumpster (*off*) Yes, Uncle Binlid.
Binlid Admiral Binlid. (*He chuckles to himself*) Dear oh, dear... I don't know though. (*He strikes a heroic pose holding a triangular piece of wreckage to his head like a cocked hat, closing one eye and putting his other hand inside his coat*) Admiral Spudskins Binlid RN... Nah, not me. I'm a land rat to the bones. (*He yawns*) Tired to the bones and all. (*He takes a quick look inside the starship*) Not much chance of Rodent and his crew waking up. Dumpster'll be gone a while. Might as well have a bit of a kip myself. (*He settles down to sleep on the floor*)

Act II

The Lights dim except for a single blue light on Binlid as at the opening

Vermin, Trash and the Guard-rats move in from the darkness

Vermin Uncle Binlid...

Trash and the Guard-rats repeat Vermin's words in a whispering echo as before

Wakey, wakey, Uncle Binlid.

"Wakey-wakey" is repeated as before

(*Loudly*) Get up!

Trash and the Guard-rats repeat "get up, get up" and flip Binlid over with their weapons

Binlid (*tumbling toward* DS) Ow!
Trash Stand and salute The Lord Vermin. Ruler of Refuse, Defender of Dumps and Guardian of Garbage.
Binlid (*sitting up*) Not another nightmare. I really got to stop eating that cheese before bedtime.
Trash Stand and show his Ratship the respect he deserves.
Binlid I can't do that, there's child-people present.
Trash Stand and salute your Lord and Master.

Trash and the Guard-rats salute Vermin as before. Binlid puts his hands to his head and waggles his fingers disrespectfully. He thumbs his nose and puts out his tongue

Vermin Guards! This has gone far enough.

Guard-rats advance on Binlid

Binlid Hey! (*He halts the Guard-rats*) This is my nightmare. I'll decide when it's gone far enough. And at the moment, I'm quite enjoying it.
Vermin You may not live to regret this, Uncle Binlid.
Binlid (*mimicking Vermin*) "You may not live to regret this." You don't frighten me, Vermin. You're just a bit of my imagination that... (*he remembers Dumpster's words*) that doesn't turn off when I go to sleep. And if I don't *imagine* you're frightening, then (*he prods Vermin as he speaks*) you ... ain't ... frightening.

Vermin is speechless with rage at being touched. Trash fusses over to dust off Binlid's fingerprints from Vermin. Vermin beats him away

> In fact, I can imagine you any way I want. I can imagine you green...

A green light shines on Vermin

> Or blue...

A blue light shines on Vermin

> Or yellow...

A yellow light shines on Vermin

> And I'm *not* frightened of you 'cos you ain't real. Come to think of it, I wouldn't be frightened of you even if you *were* real. I ain't a prisoner in your garbage. I'm a free animal. And the truth is, I always was. So there.

Dumpster, Hamilton, Bilge and Volga enter. They carry shiny metal panels each with American and Russian flags or the letters NASA and CCCP. They are stopped dead by the sight of Vermin

> Hallo, Dumpster. Welcome to my dream. You know old Vermin, don't you?

Dumpster Uncle Binlid...
Binlid Don't worry. It's just my imagination. Good, isn't it? 'Course, the real Vermin ain't quite this ugly. (*He tweaks Vermin's nose*)

Dumpster, Hamilton, Bilge and Volga stand horror-struck

> Tell you what, if it bothers you, I'll imagine he's disappeared. (*He rubs his eyes*) There you are. Gone.

Binlid looks in turn at Vermin, Trash and the Guard-rats. Each in turn waves at him to show they are still there. He realizes his mistake

> If I said I was sorry, could we just pretend this never happened?

Vermin Guards!

The Guard-rats push Dumpster, Hamilton, Bilge, Volga and Binlid DC

Binlid I just thought I'd ask.

Act II

Vermin And search their craft. See what other surprises they've "dreamed up" for us.

Trash and the Guard-rats go into the starship

I see you have a new friend.
Volga People's Laboratory Animal First Class, Volga Ratskaya. (*She salutes and begins to sing the Russian national anthem*)
Vermin (*over her singing*) How quaint. I would ask what you're all doing here. But the presence of the child-people tells me it's another misguided attempt to improve yourselves. So I'll just welcome you... BACK TO MY GARBAGE!
Volga Is not *your* garbage. Is *People's* Garbage... (*She stops to consider her own words*)
Vermin My point exactly. The grown-people have been sending things into space for over forty years. Most of it's junk now. Thousands of pieces of garbage hurtling through space with no useful purpose. So I've done a little ... recycling.
Binlid Thought you didn't approve of recycling.
Vermin Recycling is just a means to an end. It's the ends I don't approve of. I remember when your city park was a mountain of waste and rubbish. Now look at it. It's getting so a rat can't turn 'round for open space and green trees.
Hamilton It's not perfect. But it's getting better.
Dumpster That's the child-peoples' doing. That's the New Spirit.
Vermin Child-people. New Spirit. Never satisfied. Always dreaming of a better world and reaching for the stars. Well. Not for very much longer.

Trash and the Guard-rats emerge from the starship. Trash is chuckling to himself

Report.
Trash Sleeping like a baby, Your Ratship.
Vermin Who is?
Trash Captain Rodent, Your Ratship.
Bilge Admiral Rodent, actually.
Trash And all the Sea-rats. And look. (*He produces Rodent's medal*) They're all wearing them.
Vermin (*reading the inscription*) Order of the Valorous Whisker. For bravery and ingenuity in the defeat of The Lord Vermin, one time Ruler of Refuse... *One* time. Well. We can talk about that later. In the meantime, your spacecraft is just the piece of junk we've been looking for ... to blot out the last star.

Dumpster It's you. You blotted out the stars.
Vermin Yes. Child-people can't reach for the stars if they can't see them, can they? Tie them up. Tightly. They're bound to try and interfere.
Trash Oh, yes, your Ratship. Tied—bound. Bound—tied. (*He giggles*) Very funny.
Vermin Trash!
Trash (*recovering himself*) Yes, your Ratship.
Vermin We have work to do.
Trash Yes, your Ratship. Sorry, your Ratship. (*He sniggers to himself*)

Guard-rats tie Dumpster, Hamilton, Binlid, Bilge and Volga back to back with a turn of rope. Production Note: If the characters differ greatly in height then this might cause problems. Alternatively they could be tied together in line by the hand. In such case, the following action could proceed like a Mexican wave along the line of characters

Vermin That should keep you out of trouble until we return. And we will ... return.

Vermin, Trash and the Guard-rats leave

Others sit tied together DC

Binlid Well. Here's another fine mess you've got me into, Dumpster.
Dumpster Sorry, Uncle Binlid.
Bilge Cheer up. Thing's could be worse.
Binlid Why do people keep telling me that?
Volga Is wrong. Things not be vorse.
Binlid At last. Someone with a sense of reality.
Volga Is end of micht<u>art</u>. [dream]
Hamilton End of what?
Volga Is dream. I not want be Laboratory Animal. I want be ... ballet dancer.
Hamilton Ballet dancer?
Binlid I don't know. Just when I think someone's on my side, they go and turn all dreamy on me.
Volga Once I go to ballet school. I work hard. Learn steps. I show...

Volga stands to demonstrate the ballet first position. Because they are tied up, the group has to stand too. She stands in the ballet first position: basically heels together with toes pointing outwards, arms forward with palms facing body

Is first position...

Act II

Volga changes to the ballet second position: standing as before but with arms gently curved out at chest height, palms facing forward

Is second position...

Volga, from her second position, attempts to pirouette: spinning by swinging her right arm to provide the energy. The whole group is, of course, ungracefully dragged around with her

Is pirouette. (*She tries to jump gracefully into the air. Being tied up, she can't get her feet off the ground*)
Hamilton What's that?
Volga Is entrechat. Is sort of jump. (*She gives in to gravity*) Is not matter. I do...

Volga tries to demonstrate a grand plié: basically fully lowering the body by bending the knees outward from second position. The group go down with her. At the lowest point...

Aaagh...

Volga freezes rigid in pain, the others with her

Hamilton What's this position called?
Volga (*in some discomfort*) Is called cramp. I out of practice.

The group helps Volga get up as they struggle back to their collective feet

Is not matter any more. Is over. Is end of dream. I not ever dance ballet. (*She gloomily begins to hum the opening theme from Tchaikovsky's 1812 overture*)
Bilge Whiskers up, young fella. We'll soon be out of this.
Binlid Oh, yes? Well, in *your* dreams, maybe.
Hamilton Couldn't we shout and shout and shout until we wake the Admiral?
Binlid If he can sleep through the crash of the starship, he can sleep through any noise we can make.
Dumpster What do *sea rats* dream about, Mr Bilge?
Bilge Adventures mostly. Storms. Heroic rescues. That kind of thing.
Dumpster So if we could get into the Admiral's dreams...
Hamilton We could tell him we're in danger...
Binlid Then he can yawn, turn over, and go back to sleep.
Bilge No. The youngsters have got something there. What we have to do is get a signal into his subconscious.

Binlid Sub what?
Bilge The bit that doesn't turn off when he's asleep.
Binlid Oh. You mean where his dreams come from.
Bilge Yes, sir.
Binlid Then why didn't you say so? I've got a really good one of them.
Bilge All we need is the right signal. One an old sea rat just can't ignore.

Silence while they all try to think of a way to get the Admiral's attention

Dumpster How about an animal-in-distress signal!
Bilge That's it. An SOS!
Hamilton A what?
Bilge SOS. It means "Save Our Sniffers".
Hamilton Right. Let's do it. (*She shouts*) SOS. SOS. SOS...
Bilge No. We have to use a signal that'll reach into his imagination. It's a bit old-fashioned nowadays, but we'll have to use *Morse Code*.
Binlid Here. I know Morse Code. We used it when I was a nipper. Yeh. Used it to send messages 'round by squeaking down the drain pipes.
Bilge Right. Each letter has a code. And the code is made up of sounds. Either short sounds...
Binlid Like ... squeak ... squeak ... squeak. That's the code for the letter S.
Bilge Or long sounds...
Binlid Like ... squeeeeeek ... squeeeeeek ... squeeeeeek. That's the code for the letter O.
Bilge So the Morse Code for SOS is...
Binlid | (*together*)...squeak ... squeak ... squeak. (*They pause*) Squeeeeeek
Bilge | ... squeeeeeek ... squeeeeeek. (*They pause*) Squeak ... squeak ... squeak.
Bilge Quite simple, really.
Binlid But I think it'll have to be much louder to get through to the Admiral.
Dumpster Let's get the child-people to help. (*To the audience*) You'll help us wake the Admiral, won't you?

Dumpster encourages the audience to respond positively

Hamilton Yes. Let's divide into three groups, then each group can do one letter.
Bilge Right. Dumpster take the first group, Hamilton, take the third, and Volga take the middle group.

The tied-up group shuffles DR *and stands such that Dumpster faces the audience*

Act II
31

Dumpster I want all of you in this part, (*he marks the division*) to do the first S. Can you remember the Morse Code for S?

Hopefully they can

That's right, it's three short squeaks. Like this. Squeak … squeak … squeak. Let's have a practice. (*He leads the audience in squeaking*) Very good. Now don't forget that, because we're on first.

They shuffle DL and turn such that now Hamilton faces the audience

Hamilton All of you in this part, (*he marks the division*) I want you to do the last S with me. You heard them do the Morse Code for S. It's three short squeaks. Let's have a practice. (*He leads the audience in squeaking*) Right, I think they've got it.
Volga Zdr<u>a</u>stvooeetyeh. [Hallo] I vant all in this part, (*she marks the division*) do O with me. Remember Morse Code for O?

Hopefully they do

Is right. Is three long sqvveeks. So. Sqvveeeeeek … sqvveeeeeek … sqvveeeeeek. Is good. Now we practice. (*She leads the audience in "sqvveeking"*) Khurush<u>or</u>. [good] Is very good.
Bilge Well done. Let's put it all together.

They shuffle DR, turning such so that Dumpster again faces his third of the audience

Dumpster Right. Now we're relying on you. So follow us. Ready, my group? OK. After three. One—two—three… (*He leads his third*)

The tied-up group shuffles across the stage, turning as they go, so that they each face their third of the audience to lead them for the relevant code letter

Anything?
Bilge Nothing at all, I'm afraid not. Looks as though they're still sound asleep.
Binlid Better try again, only louder.
Hamilton And this time keep doing it until they wake up.
Dumpster Right. This is it. Ready? One—Two—Three… (*He again leads his third*)

The tied-up group shuffles across the stage turning and leading the audience as before. They run through the SOS once then shuffle hurriedly back to start again

Part way through this next run, the starship door opens and Rodent strolls out, yawning and stretching, followed by the Sea-rats

Rodent (*yawning*) What's all the fuss about? Someone in a spot of trouble, is it?

The tied-up group staggers around dizzy and exhausted before collapsing in a heap DC

(*Spotting the collapsed group*) Well, smoke me kippers. It's a jolly fine life for some old sea rats. Lounging around in their bunks when there's a heroic rescue in the offing. Come on, chaps, jump to it.

The Sea-rats help Dumpster, Hamilton, Binlid, Bilge and Volga to their feet and untie them

(*Seeing the rope removed by the Sea-rats*) Hmm... Looks like you chaps need a spot of rescuing yourselves. I say, wasn't *your* SOS there, was it?
Bilge Very same, sir. 'Fraid we've run into the Lord Vermin again.
Rodent Lord Vermin, eh? Thought we'd done for the jolly old rascal.
Bilge 'Fraid he very nearly did for us, sir. Till you came along, that is.
Rodent Glad to be of service, of course. Bit puzzled as to what old Vermin's doing here. Bit puzzled as to where *here* is actually. Any ideas, Mr Bilge?
Volga People's Space Research Station "Pridsta̱rveet sibby̱eh" [Imagine]. I... (*She salutes*) Laboratory Animal First Class, Volga Ratskaya. (*She begins to sing the Russian national anthem*)
Hamilton Erm... Not now, Volga. We're a bit short of time. (*She leads Volga away*)
Bilge Seems to be a derelict space station, sir.
Rodent Really? (*He sees the rocket panels*) Looks like a load of junk to me. Hazard to shipping, I shouldn't wonder.
Bilge Yes, sir. And according to Vermin, there's actually quite a lot of it.
Dumpster He's using the space junk to blot out the stars.
Rodent Well, salt me whiskers. What sort of rascally scheme is that?
Dumpster He wants to stop the child-people dreaming.
Rodent Then why doesn't he just put fleas in their beds. That'll keep them awake.
Dumpster It's not that kind of dreaming. It's eyes-open dreaming. It's imagining things. What things could be like, and how far you can go and what you might find.

Act II

Rodent Well, that's the spirit of the child-people. Always chasing stars, child-people.
Dumpster Not if they can't *see* the stars. There'll be nothing to chase. Nothing to dream about. It'll kill their spirits. It will. And Vermin knows it.
Bilge Youngsters are nothing without imagination, sir.
Rodent Well, we have a full compliment of able bodied Sea-rats now, young fella-me-rat. They've been more than a match for old Vermin before. And I imagine they can more than match the old rascal again, what?

Rodent moves DS. *As he speaks, he notices his medal is missing. He searches his pockets for it*

Unseen by him, Vermin and Trash enter and stand behind him. The Guard-rats enter from either side, surrounding the rest of the starship party and forcing them together and C

I should say so. Stealing child-peoples' dreams, is it? Well, not while Admiral Horatio Rodent's still in command. Anyone seen my dashed...

Vermin hands Rodent his missing medal

Ah. Thanks awfully, Vermin. For a minute there I thought I'd lost the jolly old gong. (*He does a complete double take*) Great rat's tails! Vermin!
Trash The Lord Vermin. (*He goes into his routine*) Ruler of the Refuse——
Vermin (*cutting in*) Admiral Rodent, I presume? Congratulations on your promotion. And on your ... little badge. Pity your next decoration will be awarded ... posthumously. Guards. Take them away and throw them into space.

The Guard-rats force the starship party DS

Rodent Steady on, Vermin. I know you're an evil tyrant and all that. Never had you down as a barbarian animal. Thought you might give a rat a fighting chance.
Vermin A fighting chance? Barbarian I may be. Fool I am not.
Dumpster How about a last meal then?
Vermin Last meal.
Dumpster Yes. Isn't that usual before an ... execution?
Vermin Very well, then. A last meal. But nothing that requires a long cooking time or sending out to a take-away.
Dumpster A little bit of cheese would be nice.
Vermin Cheese. Very well.

The Sea-rats get the smelly cheese and share it out amongst the starship party

So this is goodbye. You'll forgive me if I don't shed a tear. But you should consider yourselves honoured. Some adventurers measure their worth by the power and cunning of their enemies. And your enemy ... is the Lord Vermin.

Dumpster Yeh? Well, we measure ourselves by the courage and imagination of our friends. And our friends are the child-people. (*To the audience*) Ready? For the *New Spirit*!

The starship party join in as before, leading the audience in the countdown

FIVE ... FOUR ... THREE ... TWO ... ONE...!
Rodent PRESENT CHEESE!!

The starship party wave their cheese frantically at the audience

Binlid Deep breath... And...
Protagonists with the audience PHWORRRRR!!!
Binlid Again...
Protagonists with the audience PHWORRRRR!!!

There is a terrific sound of tearing metal. An alarm klaxon sounds. The Lights turn red and alternately brighten and dim. All stagger as if the ground is shifting. Guard-rats fall over. Sea-rats, commanded by Bilge, seize the weapons and the tables are turned

Rodent I trust there's a scientific explanation for all this noise, Mr Bilge.
Bilge Newton's Second Law, sir. When you push something, it moves according to how hard you push it. I think that last "Phworrrr" might have been a push too far.
Vermin Far too far, you fools. The space junk is falling out of orbit!
Rodent Does that mean we're going home, Mr Bilge?
Bilge Yes, sir ... at about forty thousand kilometres an hour.
Rodent Jolly good. Back in time for tea, then.
Volga Is not jolly good. Go fast too much. Vee hit atmosphere at angle less than five degree. Friction burn us to tiny cinder like shooting star. Is called Re-entry Problem.
Vermin And if the angle's greater than seven degrees, we'll bounce off into space ... for ever.
Rodent Sounds a bit tricky, Mr Bilge.
Bilge Sir.
Rodent Any idea how we steer this space junk sort of thing?
Bilge I'm afraid, sir ... we can't.
Volga Is end now. Things not ever be vorse. Is finish. (*She starts singing the 1812 theme, gloomily*)

Act II   35

Binlid Just for once I don't agree. Anyone here ride a motorcycle?
Rodent Sorry. Strictly an ocean-going rat. Always have been.
Binlid Well, just do what I do, then. Come on. This'll take every ounce of strength we got between us. Child-people too, we'll need you and all.

All line up DL *to* DR *with Binlid* DC. *This next bit looks like the emergency procedure information given by airline stewards to passengers prior to take off*

> Right. To make a motorcycle turn, you *lean* it into the corners. If you lean it to the right, it turns right. And if you lean it to the left, it turns left.
> **Rodent** Err ... what happens if you lean back?
> **Binlid** You fall off. Now. (*To the audience*) When we do this, (*he signals the audience's left*) you all lean left. And when we do this, (*he signals the audience's right*) you all lean right. Got that? Good. Now 'cos this *isn't* a motorcycle, we *can* lean forward and backward when we do this, (*he signals forward*) or this... (*He signals backward*) And just so's we get the *balance* right, we can stand up (*he signals the stand*) and sit down. (*He signals the sit*) Right, let's practice. Together... After two. One... Two...
> **All**   Lean forwards, lean backwards,
>   To the left, to the right,
>   Stand up, sit down,
>   To the left, to the right.
>   Lean forwards, lean backwards,
>   To the left, to the right,
>   Stand up, sit down,
>   To the left, to the right.

All join in giving the signals and leading the audience participation. After running through the instructions and responses once slowly, it is very easy to get the instructions into a simple rhythm/song (see music) with the audience joining in and doing all the actions. The dialogue between the two verses may also be used before singing the rhythm once more but faster

Song 3: Re-entry Song
All as chorus (*singing*) Lean forwards, lean backwards,
                   To the left, to the right,
                   Stand up, sit down,
                   To the left, to the right.
                   Lean forwards, lean backwards,
                   To the left, to the right,
                   Stand up, sit down,
                   To the left, to the right.

Bilge and Binlid sing verse 1

Bilge	Mister Binlid.
Binlid	Mister Bilge.
Bilge	I will navigate.
Binlid	But the steering, Mr Bilge.
Bilge	I will delegate.
Binlid	But what is that smell?
Bilge	I will investigate,
	Oh, yuk. It's the cheese.
Binlid	Don't worry we'll fumigate.

All as chorus (*singing*) Lean forwards, lean backwards ... (*Etc.*)

Bilge (*speaking*) We're still out of control, Mr Binlid. Better sing it again.
Binlid (*speaking*) Right, Mr Bilge. Come on, child-people. One more time. But much faster. After two. One... Two...

All as chorus (*singing*) Lean forwards, lean backwards ... (*Etc.*)

Bilge (*singing verse 2*) If you will navigate, then I will delegate.
Binlid (*joining in*) We all will congregate to steer this ship home.
        We'll co-operate, manipulate,
        Participate and anticipate,
        We'll get this ship home,
        This is starting to irritate.

All as chorus (*singing*) Lean forwards, lean backwards ... (*Etc.*)

The Lighting returns to normal and the alarm klaxon ceases

Bilge I think we're through, sir.
Dumpster You've done it. Thanks, child-people.
Volga Is now only impact to worry. (*She gloomily starts singing the 1812 theme again*)
Dumpster Impact?
Vermin Yes. At the end of this fall. And just in case you hadn't noticed, we're falling with a terminal velocity of eleven kilometres a second... Every second.
Trash Oh, yes, your Ratship. (*He giggles*) Very funny. End—terminal. Terminal——
Vermin Trash! Don't even snigger.
Trash (*recovering himself*) Yes, your Ratship.

Act II

Vermin We have to brace ourselves for impact. Every rat's life depends on the rat next to him... Or her. Even the child-people. (*To the audience*) So take a good look at the animal next to you. It may be the last face you see. Now... Link arms with the rat or child-person next to you and brace yourselves for the crash... Countdown!

All lead the audience in a countdown as before

All FIVE... FOUR... THREE... TWO... ONE...
Volga ZASTIGNOOT RYEMNEE!
Hamilton Pardon?
Volga Is fasten seatbelts.
Hamilton Oh.

There is the sound of a terribly loud crash

Black-out

The Lights slowly come back up. The starship is destroyed, pieces are scattered around the stage which is now the gardener's corner of the city park again. All the starship party and Volga are in a heap C

Vermin, Trash and the Guard-rats are not on stage

Binlid (*from somewhere in the depths of the heap of rats*) Are we dead yet?
Dumpster (*also from the depths*) Don't think so. How about you, Hamilton?
Hamilton (*from the depths*) Difficult to tell. Can you smell things when you're dead?
Dumpster Don't know. What can you smell?
Hamilton I can smell ... mouldy ... CHEESE!
All PHWORRRRR!!!

All tumble out of the heap, recover their feet and look around them

Dumpster It's the city park. We're home.
Binlid At last. Somewhere I actually want to be.
Rodent Where's that Vermin chap?
Bilge Seems he's given us the slip again, sir.
Binlid What, fancied another medal, did you?
Rodent Rather wanted to thank the old rascal, actually. Think he might have helped us out of a tight spot just there.
Binlid Well, I shouldn't worry too much. I don't imagine you've seen the last of him.

Bilge 'Fraid the *New Spirit*'s a bit of a wreck.
Binlid I think the *spirit*'s fine. Things need tidying up a bit, that's all.
Rodent Stay and give you a hand if you like.
Binlid Thanks. But I think we can manage.

Volga wanders around the stage. She looks almost disappointed to be back on Earth

Hamilton You all right, Volga? Look, it's Earth. You're home!
Volga Is not home. Is not Russia.
Hamilton It's the city park. And it's very nice. Really. And you're welcome to stay. Isn't she, Uncle Binlid?
Binlid Long as you like.
Volga Is good people. Is nice. But is not Russia. Is far from dream of ballet as in space.
Hamilton The ballet isn't everything, Volga. There's lots of other dreams you can have.
Binlid No, no, no. Don't you listen to that. If you got a dream you got to go for it. Anything less is just space junk.
Volga How is get to Russia?
Rodent Well, I'm sure we could give you a lift, if you like. 'Course, we've never been to Russia. Can't be more difficult than going to the stars though, can it, Mr Bilge?
Bilge At least it's on the map, sir.
Volga In me, Russian ballet *is* stars. (*She bear-hugs Rodent*) Spas<u>ee</u>ba [thankyou]. Ugr<u>or</u>mnaya spas<u>ee</u>ba [thank you very much]. (*She bear-hugs Bilge*)
Dumpster The stars! Do you think we saved the stars?
Binlid Can't tell at the minute. But it'll be dark soon.
Hamilton Dark soon! And I haven't slept a wink all day.
Dumpster Come on. Let's see if the stars still shine. Come on, Volga.

Dumpster, Hamilton, Volga and the Sea-rats sit to one side of the stage facing US. *Binlid, Rodent and Bilge stand* DS *to the other side. The stage gradually darkens*

Bilge And what about *your* dream, Mr Binlid? There's always room for a common-sense chap like yourself in the Rat Navy.
Rodent Be glad to put a word in for you, when we get back to port.
Binlid Can't say as I'm not tempted. But ... well, maybe when young Dumpster's up to properly looking after his self. Maybe that'll be the time for my dreams.
Bilge Very noble, sir.

Act II

Binlid After all, youngsters need something to look up to, don't they?
Bilge Very true, sir. Very true.

Stage lighting has dimmed to Black-out

There is an audible intake of breath from Hamilton, Volga and the Sea-rats as a large number of white fairy lights are turned on behind the black gauze at the back of the stage (and all over the theatre if possible). Production Note: If all this is impractical, a mirror ball would substitute

Dumpster (*whispering in wonder*) The stars!

In the darkness, all slip quietly away, leaving only the star light

The Lights come up for song and curtain call

Song 4: Space Junk Song

All
Open your eyes and
Look all around,
Look at your world with
Your feet on the ground.

Now shut your eyes and
Imagine you see,
Imagine your world
As you'd like it to be.

This starry bright world's not
As far as it seems,
If you don't let the junk
Hide the light of your dreams.

CURTAIN

The Wonder Of It All
Dumpster - Hamilton

Cue: **Hamilton** ...I'm afraid it might get broken hanging around up here.

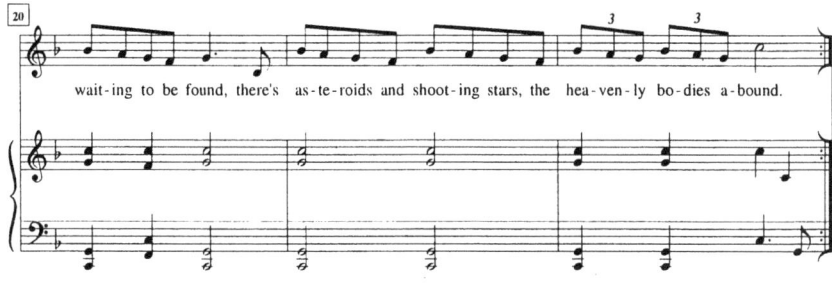

Volga's Song
Volga

Cue: **Hamilton** I had a wheel like that once.
Someone oiled the axle. I just
couldn't stop it.

The Re-Entry Song
Bilge - Binlid - Everyone

Cue: **Hamilton** Right let's practice.
Together, after 2, 1... 2...

Space Junk
Everyone

FURNITURE AND PROPERTY LIST

Further dressing may be added at the director's discretion

ACT I

On stage: 2 outsize plant pots
Gardening paraphernalia
Sign: "City Free Park"
Sign: "Please take your litter home"
Seed tray
Oversize alarm clock

Off stage: Pointed weapons—oversize cocktail sticks, pencils or cutlery (**Guard-rats**)
Boat made from sardine tin. *In it*: **Binlid**'s smashed alarm clock (**Sea-rats** and **Bilge**)
Megaphone (**Rodent**)
Outsize pieces of rubbish (**Sea-rats**)
Lumps of very ripe cheese (**Bilge** and **Sea-rats**)
Silvery suits (**Dumpster** and **Hamilton**)

Personal: **Dumpster:** twigs and leaves stuck in clothes
Hamilton: night cap
Rodent: orders, map, medal
Sea-rats: medals

ACT II

On stage: Starship upside-down
Cheese

Off stage: Weapons (**Guard-rats**)
Shiny metal panels each with American and Russian flags or the letters NASA and CCCP (**Dumpster, Hamilton, Bilge** and **Volga**)

Personal: **Trash: Rodent**'s medal
Guard-rats: rope

LIGHTING PLOT

Property fittings required: nil
2 exterior settings

ACT I

To open:	Blue light overhead on **Binlid**	
Cue 1	**Vermin** stands on upturned seed tray *Red light overhead on* **Vermin**	(Page 2)
Cue 2	**Binlid**: "No, please... Aaaah!" *Black-out*	(Page 3)
Cue 3	**Dumpster**: "Aaaah!" *Bring lights up*	(Page 3)
Cue 4	**Sea-rats** enter with pieces of rubbish *Dim lights* US	(Page 10)
Cue 5	**Rodent**: "...no rat's been bold enough to go." *Bring up lights* US	(Page 11)
Cue 6	**All**: "Phwor!!" *Bring up gently pulsating light*	(Page 15)
Cue 7	Rocket motor grows steadily louder *Increase pulsating light*	(Page 15)
Cue 8	Rocket motor reaches full volume *Black-out; when ready bring up light on starship interior*	(Page 16)
Cue 9	**Dumpster** and **Hamilton** wander DS *Fade up lights* DS, *fade down lights* US	(Page 16)
Cue 10	**Hamilton**: "At least not yet." *Sweeping spotlight*	(Page 16)

Space Junk

Cue 11	**Dumpster**: "You are clever, Hamilton." *Cut sweeping spotlight*	(Page 16)
Cue 12	**Hamilton** and **Dumpster** sit on edge of stage *Dim lights* DS, *fade up on inside of starship* US	(Page 17)
Cue 13	Deafening crash *Flash lights quickly and brightly, then black-out; when ready, bring up lights on starship*	(Page 19)

ACT II

Cue 14	**Dumpster, Hamilton** and **Bilge** turn to look behind *Black-out*	(Page 20)
Cue 15	**Dumpster, Hamilton** and **Bilge** turn back *Bring up lights*	(Page 20)
Cue 16	**Dumpster, Hamilton** and **Bilge** turn to look behind *Black-out*	(Page 21)
Cue 17	**Dumpster, Hamilton** and **Bilge** turn back *Bring up lights*	(Page 21)
Cue 18	**Binlid** settles down to sleep on floor *Fade lights down except for blue spot on* **Binlid**	(Page 24)
Cue 19	**Binlid**: "I can imagine you green…" *Green spot on* **Vermin**	(Page 26)
Cue 20	**Binlid**: "Or blue…" *Blue spot on* **Vermin**	(Page 26)
Cue 21	**Binlid**: "Or yellow…" *Yellow spot on* **Vermin**	(Page 26)
Cue 22	**Vermin**: "Guards!" *Snap off yellow spot, bring up stage lights*	(Page 26)
Cue 23	**All**: "PHWORRRRR!!!" *Turn lights red, alternately brighten and dim*	(Page 34)

Lighting Plot

Cue 24	End of *Re-Entry Song* *Return lights to normal*	(Page 36)
Cue 25	Very loud crash *Black-out; slowly bring lights up*	(Page 37)
Cue 26	**Dumpster, Hamilton, Volga** and **Sea-rats** sit *Gradually fade lights down*	(Page 38)
Cue 27	**Bilge**: "Very true, sir. Very true." *Fade to black-out; fade up back drop star effect*	(Page 39)
Cue 28	**All** exit *Bring up lights*	(Page 39)

EFFECTS PLOT

ACT I

Cue 1	To open *Clock ticks; multiply when ready, follow with alarm clock ringing loudly, and others of different types*	(Page 1)
Cue 2	**Trash** throws alarm clock off *Crash off*	(Page 1)
Cue 3	**Bilge** and **Sea-rats** enter *Sea-shanty music*	(Page 5)
Cue 4	**All**: "Phwor!!" *Sound of rocket motor*	(Page 15)
Cue 5	**All**: "PHWORRRRR!!!" *Rocket motor, louder*	(Page 15)
Cue 6	**Binlid** goes into starship *Rocket motor at full volume*	(Page 16)
Cue 7	**Binlid** and **Rodent** stand looking at a map *Fade rocket noise*	(Page 16)
Cue 8	**Hamilton**: "At least not yet." *Cyclic rushing noise*	(Page 16)
Cue 9	**Dumpster**: "You are clever, Hamilton." *Cut rushing noise*	(Page 16)
Cue 10	**All** put fingers in ears *Deafening and prolonged crash, then silence*	(Page 19)

Effects Plot

ACT II

Cue 11	**All**: "PHWORRRRR!!!" *Terrific sound of tearing metal; alarm klaxon*	(Page 34)
Cue 12	End of *Re-Entry Song* *Cut alarm klaxon*	(Page 36)
Cue 13	**Hamilton**: "Oh." *Terribly loud crash*	(Page 37)

www.ingramcontent.com/pod-product-compliance
Ingram Content Group UK Ltd.
Pitfield, Milton Keynes, MK11 3LW, UK
UKHW021847210426
5322IPUK00022B/524